ਜਗੁ ਸੁਪਨਾ ਬਾਜੀ ਬਨੀ ਖਿਨ ਮਹਿ ਖੇਲੁ ਖੇਲਾਇ ॥

'The world is a drama, staged in a dream. In a moment, the play is played out.'
Guru Nanak Dev Ji, Sri Guru Granth Sahib Ji
(Ang 18 -8)

PART ONE: You

PART TWO: The Flow

PART THREE: Mother Nature

ACKNOWLEDGMENTS

Them that I know, know that I love them...

There are so many people in my life that I could name individually that have supported my growth and given me the encouragement to share my content.

Thank you for being a part of the ups, the downs and all that is yet to come.

My deepest gratitude goes to Jasdip Sensi for all his efforts in designing the cover.

FOREWORD

The central vision of this book came about during daily commutes to work pre-pandemic. Many of you can understand the joys of tube delays and the tendency to look down at your phone to avoid eye contact, whilst travelling on the London Underground. We are often stereotyped for being an unfriendly bunch, especially on the trains. For me however, it was very much looking down at my phone on the notes section of my iPhone, writing down my observations of the world in a metaphorical way.

This book is very much a personal steppingstone in my own journey... a gift to myself for entering my thirties. I would very much describe myself as someone who enjoys digging deeper and finding hidden meanings in everything that surrounds us. There is always a positive to be found, only if you look closely. I hope you enjoy the view of the world from my perspective...quite literally. It is to be hoped that this book inspires you and helps you self-reflect on your own journey, wherever you are, wherever you are headed and whatever stage of life you are at.

For more content, follow:

Instagram:
@horizonperspective

WordPress:

@horizonperspective

PART ONE

You

APPRECIATION

We often become so entrenched within our own individual journeys that we forget to appreciate what we already have. Greed can most often define our attitude. Without even realising, we get caught up in a vicious cycle of continuously wanting more. We set our expectation levels so high that when they are not met, we feel enraged and drawn away from those around us and everyday life. Eventually forming a cycle of wanting and seeking more. This very cycle takes away appreciation and without appreciation we quite simply become vultures.

Sometimes it is essential to step away and assess your life from an outsider's perspective. We as humans have a natural tendency to want more and this is not always a bad thing. 'More' may be in the form of physical possessions or more may be in the form of a constant pursuit to find "happiness". The temporary 'fulfilment' we get from these things makes us overlook simplicity and all the ordinary things that surround us. These may be our support circles, those who are near and dear to us. We forget the importance of these people within our lives, the very concept of wanting more has us constantly looking for happiness in every other place. We get caught up in this cycle where we end up losing the value of life and even losing sense of self. Ultimately, we define our own happiness and we do not really need much searching because happiness can be found in the here and now with the most minimum of things.

INDIVIDUALITY

In a society driven by social media and a constant need for validation, we are often left questioning who we truly are. We may feel the need to join the crowd and adapt who we are in order to be socially accepted. Our very sense of individuality appears to be eroding as we try and conform to this social concept of normality.

The real question is, without even realising why do so many of us fear deviating from this social concept of normality? We as individuals find a constant need to dress a certain way or behave a certain way in order to gain social acceptance and provide ourselves with validation. By doing so we often lose our sense of individuality. We are quite easy to forget who we truly are and what we have to offer, as we become so focused on being like everyone else. Nobody can be you and that's probably the closest thing we'll get to having a superpower (for now anyway).

We all have our individual flaws but if we fail to embrace them then we prevent ourselves from growing as individuals. Masking ourselves in order to be like everyone else will not make us happy. Happiness is an inside job and starts and ends with you alone. Sometimes we just need to take out some time to celebrate ourselves and who we are and what we bring to the table. In a garden full of flowers each flower brings its own colour and adds its own value. Regardless of its colour, its growth and its smell, it will always try to firmly hold its place amongst the other flowers, be it rain or shine.

Next time you doubt your own self -worth remember who you truly are and what you're capable of. Don't let society dictate who and what you should be. Why be like everyone else?

DETOX

What we see of the world is largely based upon what we give focus to. If we constantly see negativity around us and give focus to negativity, we mentally clog our minds with such thoughts. People often detox their bodies to cleanse their insides. Similarly, our minds and souls need detoxing too! It's easy to get caught up within the hustle and bustle of life. Sometimes we need a break and need to focus on our mental well-being, to keep us sane in this forever fast-moving world.

So, how exactly can we detox the soul? Firstly, we can start by removing any excess baggage within our souls, it's easy to overthink situations and replay past scenarios. Every experience the good, the bad and the ugly serves as an experience. Experiences act as learning curves for the future. We should learn to accept the present day as a blessing and take each day as it comes. Dwelling in the past simply takes up unnecessary mind space. Every so often we need to find a way to declutter our thoughts and free up that space.

We can also detox mentally by removing ourselves or avoiding situations that consume unnecessary energy. If something or someone constantly drains your energy you may need to find a way to eliminate it. It'll probably help clear your mind and help keep you better focused on your own personal progression. The less we respond to negativity the more peaceful our lives can become.

Cleanse out the toxins occasionally, not just in the body but in the mind and soul too. Declutter your thoughts, cleanse your soul and destress your mind.

GRATITUDE

Covid-19 has impacted us all to a great degree. The year of 2020 and the beginning of 2021 has been life changing for all of us. Many of us have been in and out of lockdowns, all around the world. Though in the larger scale of things, these lockdowns were just temporary situations, they became a time of reflection and appreciating all that surrounded us.

It all still feels rather surreal looking back on the pandemic. During the pandemic, we had to all embrace uncertainty and pace ourselves to take on each day as it came. As the world around us began to slow down, we learnt how to adjust to the new ways of life during the pandemic. For many of us this meant creating new routines and learning new ways of life.

Practicing gratitude during these challenging times was essential. The news would report daily increases and place heavy emphasis upon the uncertainty this pandemic had caused. For many, this period was daunting and heart-breaking. From losing jobs, losing loved ones, long queues at supermarkets, no one really knew when this would come to an end and when life would return to 'normal'. The biggest lesson from the pandemic for me personally was learning the art of gratitude. With so much going on in the world, it became easy to forget the importance of the little things. As humans, we always naturally want more in every area of our lives.

The pandemic clearly demonstrated how the little things were what mattered the most. These included: being alive, having shelter, having an income, having food and being able to connect with family and friends. 'More' at this stage was not an option. Simple gestures such as hugging became precious gifts during the pandemic. With limited social contact and physical contact, we could only really rely upon technology and words alone to express love and gratitude to loved ones. Prior to the lockdown we would take such things for granted because everything was readily available, without restrictions and limitations.

In hindsight, gratitude in this sense can not only help us appreciate the difficulties of the past but can help bring an element of peace for today and provide us with resilience for the future. Practising gratitude daily can help us appreciate all the things we have and often overlook. It can help us feel more fulfilled within our day to day lives and pace us in our journey.

As Melody Beattie quite rightly puts it:

'Gratitude turns what we have into enough'.

VISION

No matter how brilliant your eyesight may be, quite often we are simply the own cause of blurring our vision. It is easy to let the past control the future, but we must stop and get ourselves to start seeing things more clearly. Take control of the mind fog!! Mind fog can be considered as all those little things that congest our mind. A cloud of pollution that prevents us from seeing things for all they are. This is all metaphorically speaking of course!

In order to attain this 'perfect vision' where exactly do we start? Here's my top three suggestions:

Clarify your vision:

For those of us who wear glasses you will almost certainly understand the pain of having rain droplets steam up your glasses. Pretty frustrating right? Blurred vision? That is literally it! Regardless, with and without glasses, it is quite often essential to refocus your vision. Sometimes we look but we do not actually see. Let's explore that sentence a little more. We can often look past everything that surrounds us because we are so focused on the past or planning for the future. It is like we exist, but are we actually make the most of our time here? This is exactly why it is important to clarify our vision, quite often we are the cause of the blurriness. We need not only to look but to actually see.

We can do this by first looking at ourselves and figuring out who we are as individuals. A process of reflection can help us figure out exactly what and how we can better develop ourselves and what we hope to achieve. Set some targets and goals for yourself to help you grow and step out of comfort zones. Self-focusing accompanied with growth can help clarify your vision. Pave your own road and take active steps towards achieving what you seek.

Decluttering Decisions:

As important as it is to declutter unwanted things around us it is just as important to declutter the mind. Clear the clutter, make some space for what is important. As Maria Kondo quite rightly puts it "discard everything that does not spark joy". It is easier said than done but sometimes it is essential to remove stuff that no longer serves a purpose from both our mind and physical surroundings. This helps us simplify life by creating space and time for things that matter. By doing so we begin to see things a lot more clearly for what they are instead of what we imagine them to be.

Mind Fuel:

In order for us to see things clearly, we need mind fuel. It is essential to snap out of our tech savvy world here and there. Find yourself a good book to read to fuel your thoughts. Go for a walk and immerse yourself in nature. Nature can help you destress and make you feel a lot more present and grounded. In chapter three of this book, you can discover more about mother nature.

Ultimately, we are a product of our own thoughts. Sometimes it is as simple as waking up every day with the thought that something wonderful is about to happen. With this logic you'll learn to find "wonderful" in the simplest of things. Expressing gratitude can help us refuel our mind.

Those are my three suggestions to help you attain a somewhat clearer vision. Hold the vision and trust the process. Create the highest vision for yourself, for if you believe it – you will be sure to achieve i

ALIGNMENT

We often find the need to speed up life, in every area we can. Not only may societal pressures be the cause of this but we ourselves often become our biggest critics. The universe, however, has bigger and better plans for us. Whether you believe in God or not there is surely a superpower up there who protects us and aligns everything for us. From the people we encounter, to the lessons we learn and the milestones we achieve, this has all been aligned individually for each one of us.

Coming from a millennial generation I often find a lot of people have a mindset of always wanting the next best thing. A mindset in which being ahead of each other is an achievement of some sort. If anything, we should all be cheering each other on. A circle of support will help you all win at life. You're only competition should be yourself. There is no set age to do anything. Nobody is you and nobody has a right to judge your journey. You can get caught up in a world of comparisons but ultimately you hold your own paint brush, and your canvas is still an artwork. Even if there's scribbles everywhere and if the strokes are not so tidy and neat, it is still art. Life cannot be and will not be perfect. We all have gloomy days. Wherever you are in your journey trust it, for one day it will make sense.

The positioning of our life is exactly where it is meant to be. We may often find ourselves diving into the past or questioning the future. That is ok, if you pause and think about the here and now. You will figure it all out, at the right time. Realign your energy.

SELF- LOVE

'How do you spell love?'- Piglet.
'You don't spell it, you feel it'- Pooh.

Love. Like Pooh says you feel it. Love is a feeling. Love can also be seen through actions. How much of that love do you feel for you? In the midst of loving everyone else, we can quite often forget ourselves.

That's right you. Yes, You. You need to feel some of your own love to get you through. Sometimes we fail and sometimes we win. Regardless, always give yourself a pat on the back. You have to learn to embrace all the different pieces of your own puzzle. They all fit together to make you who you are. You're allowed to be a work in progress!

How can we attain self-love? Well, here's my take on it.

Prioritise you:

You matter, you're loved, and you're allowed to make mistakes. It's ok to have a hard day, you don't have to knock yourself down. Just get back up and try again. Progression will help you find the best version of you. Give back to yourself. You need time to nourish yourself.

Pamper yourself:

Everything that brings you comfort, go seek it! Whether it's hitting the gym, eating pizza, watching movies snuggled in a blanket or learning new things. No matter what stage of life you're at, you can always try and fit some time in for yourself. Even if it's five mins! It'll work wonders. Self-care will help you refocus your energy.

Boundaries:

Set some boundaries. Stay away from toxic cycles, negativity or drama that drains you. You know yourself best. If something doesn't feel right, you'll almost certainly feel it. Keep a distance and focus on yourself. If you were sat on a table full of rotten food, you wouldn't want to consume it. Save your energy and mind power for you. Feed the brain selectively. Stay away from the things and people that drain you.

Be you:

You're at your own stage in life. Try not to compare yourself to be like everyone else. What's meant for you will find you. Pace yourself and embrace your own journey. It's not a competition. Each stage in life will reveal a different version of you. All these versions combined are what make you unique. It's easy to have racing thoughts wondering what the future holds in store but the only person that will get you through it all is you! So, appreciate yourself as you are and have faith in what you'll become.

Those are my top four suggestions in attaining self-love. Always remember to value yourself and embrace the journey!

PART TWO

The Flow

ENERGY

You are probably thinking this post entails a list of energy drinks to give you a boost and make you fly (I can only try). Fortunately, for you this is not a Red Bull promotion, but we can still find a way to make good energy fly!

Let us think about this in a metaphorical manner. We live in this big puffy bubble where we float around in our day to day lives. Quite often we come across circumstances that can easily hinder our floating ways (in normal terms our daily envisions, goals etc) essentially popping our puffy bubble. Your energy is ultimately a reflection of you. In order to survive in this chaotic world, we must protect our bubble by creating positive energy. This can be done by continuously striving to achieve our goals despite the setbacks and striving to better ourselves. If we fuel ourselves with positive energy, we give off that energy in turn to everyone around us, helping to better each other. Hey, it is a contagious circle!

If you give out positive energy it will often come back to you in some form or another. The energy you give off does not lie, we radiate our energy and quite often our intuition tells us when something is not right. In this case if something feels off it most probably is, trust the gut and keep moving. When you understand someone's energy you probably will not need to question their intentions. In essence the energy we give off pretty much introduces us before we even speak.

Keep giving the world good energy and protect your own energy. As Aristotle quite rightly states:

"The energy of your mind is the essence of your life-" Aristotle

TRAIN TRACKS

The time was 7:35 am, I stood patiently at the overground platform waiting for my train at the station. As I observed the queue of commuters waiting on the platform opposite and beside me, I had a thought … train tracks. Train tracks can essentially be viewed as a metaphor for our lives. Sometimes we can be the train itself and sometimes we're the tracks. How and why, you may wonder?

We often intend to board a train with a destination in mind but sometimes that does not go to plan, this may be due to the serious delays or signal failures along the way (pretty common with in London with TfL). Similarly, we are the train in our own life, we try and pursue certain pathways with a goal in mind. However, life does not always go to plan, and we may face several setbacks before we reach our destination, but we will eventually find a way to get there! It's like missing one train but another one will almost certainly follow. In this sense there will always be another opportunity to get on board again with our goals. Maybe it will be an even better experience, or an even better opportunity. You may even get a comfortable seat on the next train instead of standing all the way on the missed train.

Train tracks can be seen as the paths our lives follow. Much like the tracks our lives have already been coordinated, everything has already been written. What is meant for you will be for you. Just like the long queue of commuters waiting along the platform to board the train, we have a long queue of people within our lives, some who we have met, some who we are yet to meet. Every person we meet is positioned in our lives to teach us something. Some of them stay, some of them leave and some just pass by. Some may bring us happiness; others may bring us pain and some help teach us valuable life lessons. The people we meet ultimately shape our

13

experiences of the world and make us become who we are. Much like trains, they still go under tunnels despite the rain and despite the sun. Regardless of the weather and the number of people getting on and off, the train has a destination to reach, and it will keep moving.

There's always a light at the end of the tunnel no matter how dark it may seem. Just like our lives no matter the setbacks we have to find a way to strive and become the best possible version of ourselves. Align your tracks and follow them through. Just remember to keep those close who wait with you until the train comes, they're worth keeping on board.

MOTION

Sometimes life may slow us down and we may feel like we're going backwards instead of forwards. We need to remember that life is always in motion so you can't really be stuck. Our mind ultimately controls what we give power to. We can undo our thoughts of moving backwards and program them to move forwards. This may not be an easy task, but every day is a chance for us to reinvent ourselves and take active steps to flow with life. We can make our life a miracle in slow motion.

Progression can't really be measured through motion. Take for example a rocking horse it'll keep moving but it won't really progress anywhere. So, no matter how fast we move or how slow we move, we ultimately require a strong mental mind set to help us progress. The actions taken by both our mind and body will help pull us through any given situation. Both motion and progress require movement, but motion alone won't get you to your destination. Being persistent will help us stay in motion.

Regardless of what happened yesterday life will keep moving. The sea will keep flowing, the sun will keep rising, time will keep ticking and nothing will ever stay still. Just like the waves of the ocean change depending on the wind and the weather, we have to keep things moving despite the setbacks or achievements. All things are constant movement. We just have to keep moving with the flow. Maybe that's the secret.

THE ORDINARY

As humans we often seek to escape the ordinary in search for the extraordinary. Whilst it is essential to strive for the very best it is also important to have value in the ordinary. The ordinary is what makes the extra-ordinary.

In today's society we have tendency to want more, and we quite often forget to appreciate the simple things in life and what we already have. We may find ourselves spending most of our working weeks waiting for the next weekend. Spending most of our working days waiting for our next big holiday. Though it's important to plan and anticipate what's to come, we often lose sight of joy in the ordinary. Whilst waiting for the next weekend, we forget to appreciate the day-to-day routines which make us who we are. Whilst waiting for our next big holiday, we forget to appreciate having an income which is what allows us to afford the luxuries in life.

Regardless of what happened yesterday life will keep moving. The sea will keep flowing, the sun will keep rising, time will keep ticking and nothing will ever stay still. Just like the waves of the ocean change depending on the wind and the weather, we have to keep things moving despite the setbacks or achievements. All things are constant movement. We just have to keep moving with the flow. Maybe that is the secret.

In a generation with limitless opportunities, we get lost in a cycle of wanting more and needing more. During this cycle we forget to appreciate some of the simplest things around us including life itself. As cliche as it sounds every day is a gift. Being content will help us find joy in the now. From having people around, us who make us happy, to having routines which give our life structure and challenges which help us grow. All these things are what make life ordinary yet so extraordinary. Sometimes we find ourselves searching for the highs of life without realising what's right in front of us. Appreciate the now and the little things life has to offer. Go find joy in the ordinary.

KINTSUGI

Kintsugi? What is it? It's a Japanese term which translates to mean "golden joinery". It's often used to describe the process of fixing broken pottery, by mending the cracks with either gold or silver dust. This process of repairing the pottery not only adds value to the broken object but highlights the cracks that still hold it together. We can learn something from this very concept and apply it to life.

The art of embracing the cracks can help us view the setbacks, failures and traumas in our life from a different perspective. We all have low points and when we're going through them, we don't always believe in ourselves. Ultimately our ability to deal with these low points, helps shape who we are and who we become in the future. Often when dealing with setbacks, we may find ourselves cracking within that's metaphorically speaking. Not only does this impact our attitude towards life in general but it can further create fears within us that can lead to us question who we are and what we seek. This is where we can use the concept of kintsugi to fill in the cracks with gold dust! Not quite literally gold dust but we can use the power of positive thinking and self-reassurance to help fill in these intricate cracks within ourselves, from wherever they appear.

Though each crack comes with its own intricacies, we can put ourselves back together in a way that will make us stronger. If we put aside time and energy to heal ourselves, we eventually will. Just as the Japanese reinforce the breaks in the ceramics using gold dust, we are allowed to show our scars as we triumph our way through life. Life will inevitably come with adversity, it's all about growing through it, whilst we truly discover who we are and the power we hold within ourselves.

The next time you feel defeated or broken, try and fill your cracks with gold.

JIGSAWS

1 hour later we had only managed to fit 10 pieces together. Every Christmas me and my family attempt to finish a jigsaw puzzle (the completion of the puzzle that's another story!). Whilst playing around with each individual piece by rotating it and finding its perfect fit, it made me realise much of our journeys through our lives are like jigsaw puzzles.

Our day-to-day experiences may sometimes feel like disconnected pieces. It's often easy to forget the bigger picture as with a puzzle and as with life. Each experience helps us develop within ourselves and creates new learning windows within us. These learning windows in turn help us see the bigger picture, maybe not immediately but perhaps in the foreseeable future. Many of the disconnected experiences or so to say pieces are unknowingly connected for our own self development. The most important part of the jigsaw is us. Who we are as individuals and what we bring?

Much like jigsaw pieces we all have our "fitted" place. You may never know where you fit but others will require that little piece of you in their puzzle to help them complete, they're jigsaw. Sometimes there's no sense of wholeness or completion but each piece is a part of something not yet revealed. Ultimately the final picture is already created we just have to experience each disconnected piece to one day assemble the connected image as a whole.

Next time you pick up a jigsaw maybe you'll see it differently! If you do happen to pick up a piece that looks like the sky but when rotated, it's the ocean apply that perspective to life. Sometimes we just need to keep an open mind the answers are right in-front of us.

PART THREE

Mother Nature

SUNSETS

What are the primary colours of a sunset? What time does the sun even set? An everyday occurrence that holds the power to capture so many of us around the world. You can never have enough pictures of the sunset on your camera roll, no matter where you are. Sunsets are pretty much the sky flaunting its beauty and speaking in a thousand colours.

This everyday natural occurrence can help us understand the timings of life. No matter how difficult your day has been, the day itself will ultimately come to an end. Though the hardships of the day may continue tomorrow, we can use the sunset to help us mentally prepare our steps ahead.

So how would you describe the feeling of watching a sunset? To me, personally, it's like unconditional warmth, a big hug from nature and better still liberation from the day. There's an enigmatic beauty about daylight fading and darkness arising. Darkness covered by moonlight, pretty much the reflection of the sun. The shift between sunlight and moonlight can help us reiterate the process of self-reflection. The need to slow down and dim our energy accordingly. Just like the sun needs to set and provoke moonlight (a reflection of itself) we need to ensure we use this moment to provoke reflection within ourselves. Relax and reflect on the day and better still what's ahead.

Lastly, the very best thing about sunsets… they are free, and you can view them every day, no matter where you are.

TREES

Trees? Yes! A page dedicated to trees (though the pages in this book are probably compiled from a wonderful tree somewhere out there). Let's start with the basics, trees are made of several components, for now we'll focus on the main ones: roots, branches and leaves.

For a tree to stand tall and essentially to survive, it needs strong roots. The roots help keep the tree grounded, holding its place firmly within the soil. Similarly, as humans for us to gain a better understanding of ourselves, we need to establish our roots, who we are and what we are? The mind is our key root, the roots not only help keep us grounded with life but also test our resilience. The deeper our roots the more resilient we learn to become. Just like trees we need to learn to thrive through every season withstanding every obstacle that comes our way. This may be easier said than done but resilience can help give us the power to water our very core root which is the mind. Those near and dear to us can also help strengthen our roots, especially those who help keep us grounded when times get difficult and provide us with that extra strength to get through the not so bright seasons. Find your roots and stand tall!

Branches also rely upon the very roots of the tree to help them grow. The more branches on the tree the bigger the growth. As humans we can also branch out our roots. Find ways of branching out your mind by learning and developing new skills for yourself. Every branch within our lives can help us develop and diversify ourselves whilst strengthening our mind.

With branches come leaves! Leaves change colour with the seasons and fly with the wind. Our experiences in life can be viewed as the leaves. We can learn to view every day in a more radiant and bright coloured way. Every day comes with its own challenges. Sometimes we have to learn to persevere despite the setbacks. A piece of art isn't created overnight, the artist has to work on it day in and day out, continuous efforts help create the final masterpiece. As with a tree it requires sunshine, water and nutrients for it to stand tall and give us oxygen. Find your roots, stay grounded and keep growing!

21

NUBVIGANT

Nubvigant? It is a word! A word I discovered a while ago and thought it quite accurately described my fascination with clouds. So, what does nubvigant mean? Nubvigant is defined as an obsolete adjective which essentially means to wander through the clouds- moving through the air.

Let us tie the region of the upper air i.e., the clouds to the sky. Quite often people say the sky is the limit. Is the sky really the limit? Maybe the limit is in your mind and not in the sky. Maybe we can use the sky and the clouds to envision the limitless sea of opportunities that surround us whilst we're grounded. The act of being nubvigant can help us paint our own sky, create our very own canvas. You do not need the clouds to disappear to see a brighter day you can still envision it as a brighter day, it's all open to our own personal interpretation.

Nature can quite often be a form of escapism especially being part of a society lost in technology and social media. So, the next time you take a stroll, try and be more present in your surroundings and look up at the clouds! Use them as source of inspiration. They shift and they drift and may appear in all sorts of changing shapes, but our interpretation defines them. The changes in shape can serve as a reminder, to embrace the changes in our life and to keep flowing and growing. Keep wandering, keep drifting, keep shifting.

SPIDERS WEB

10pm... I entered the toilet with a reading book in hand. Sorry for over sharing but it's an essential back story! 10:05pm... I see a spider crawling along its web, at the very bottom of the wall. Ahh it's ok I thought, it won't quite reach the top or anywhere near to me. Not anytime soon. 10:08pm panic mode! The spider creeps its way up the wall, aligned its legs to get around the corner and sits right above my head. 10:10pm... one of its legs slips and it falls all the way down. Panic over.

Despite it being quite unfortunate the spiders climb came to an end so soon, it was symbolic of many of the daily encounters we face in life. We often let failure set us back but forget to realise all we've learnt along the way. The spiders journey up the wall may not have been easy but the very process of getting up there meant success in this sense is attainable. Sometimes falling back down is an essential step in our journeys, to remind us that getting back up there can be done. It paves the way for a new climb whilst humbling us.

The next time things in your life don't go as planned remember the spiders journey up the web. For a spiders speciality lies in building its web, regardless of how many times it falls it continues weaving and climbing. Detangle the sense of failure and change your mindset to retry climbing the delicate pathways life has set out for you. The fall itself is crucial in order for us to discover what lays at the very bottom. So, the next time we do climb back up, we remember to express gratitude in the journey itself, even if we do make it to the very top.

PETRICHOR

Have you ever smelt that earthy smell after it's rained? There's a term for it and that term is petrichor. Pretty much meaning the wonderful smell (for some) in the air after it's just rained. Being born and bought up in London has meant learning to love the rain.

Rain is often considered to symbolise darkness more so in the literary context. The term petrichor places rain in a slightly different limelight. That earthy smell quite naturally helps us refocus on the here and now, providing us with an element of gratitude in that we have the natural ability to smell, breathe and think for ourselves. Rain in the form of raindrops can help serve a reminder that we all fall and we all land somewhere. A fall doesn't necessarily have to mean failure. A fall with a sense of landing can create a whole world of opportunities. Sometimes we just have to jump in the puddles.

The next time you find yourself caught in the rain (hopefully with an umbrella) or even watching the rain from afar, let it rejuvenate you. Not only do living organisms require rain for survival and growth, but we can also use the rain to help us reflect on our own individual journey. Rain can help bring peace of mind and joy, it all really depends on you and how you look at it.

DISCONNECT

60 seconds…one minute. 24 hours…one day.
How much of that time do you spend on you? Away from the technology? Away from the distractions of day-to-day life? Put away your phone, stop the scrolling, turn off the tv and reconnect with yourself. Close all the mental tabs open in your brain. In a generation that's always on the move, it's essential to slow down the time for no other than you.

With technology all around us it's hard to disconnect. Take for example your Wi-Fi goes down or your phone has no signal, how agitated do you feel? I know for one I'm the first to wave about my phone to get a connection from somewhere. Whilst connections are what keep us going and are essential within our lives, sometimes it's important to simply disconnect. How exactly do we disconnect? It is quite simple; it is a free process that is available to us all. Look around you. Go for a walk. We are quite often consumed within our day to day lives that we forget to immerse ourselves in our everyday surroundings and feel present within the here and now.

Mother Nature can certainly help you attain that level of disconnection. Reacquainting with nature can help you appreciate stillness. The next time you're on a walk maybe practice the fours S's - Stop, Smell, See and Surround. Each of these in turn can help you feel present and embrace the pace of nature. The pace of nature can help serve a reminder that slowing down is not always a bad idea but is essential in order to promote growth, development and a state of solitude. The secret to nature is patience, take for example a caterpillar. After spending most of its time in a cocoon, with patience and science it transforms into a beautiful butterfly.

Though, we may not grow wings physically, we can mentally use nature to help slow us down and reconnect with ourselves on a deeper level. Disconnecting every now and again will lead you to a path of self-discovery and mental stillness. So, before you close this book, turn over the page and disconnect from my perspectives (quite literally) maybe use those 60 seconds to observe your senses and your surroundings. What sounds can you hear? Maybe go wonder where the Wi-Fi is weak, amongst the trees and let the silence of nature speak louder than the words and tabs open in your brain.

Disconnect…

Printed in Great Britain
by Amazon